T0030881

Farrar Straus Giroux Books for Young Readers
An imprint of Macmillan Publishing Group, LLC
120 Broadway, New York, NY 10271
mackids.com

Text copyright © 2022 by Audrey Ades
Pictures copyright © 2022 by Adelina Lirius
All rights reserved.

Our books may be purchased in bulk for promotional, educational, or business use. Please contact your local bookseller or the Macmillan Corporate and Premium Sales Department at (800) 221-7945 ext. 5442 or by email at MacmillanSpecialMarkets@macmillan.com.

Library of Congress Cataloging-in-Publication Data is available.

First edition, 2022
Color separations by Embassy Graphics
Printed in China by RR Donnelley Asia Printing Solutions Ltd., Dongguan City, Guangdong Province

ISBN 978-0-374-31476-7 (hardcover)
10 9 8 7 6 5 4 3 2 1

The art for this book was created digitally using Procreate, with some elements painted traditionally with gouache. The text was set in Cosmiqua Regular and Raphael, and the display type was created by the illustrator. Designed by Melisa Vuong, with art direction by Aram Kim. Production was supervised by John Nora, and the production editors were Allyson Floridia and Helen Seachrist. Edited by Grace Kendall, with support from Elizabeth Lee.

I Am Mozart, Too

The Lost Genius of Maria Anna Mozart

Words by
Audrey Ades

Pictures by
Adelina Lirius

Farrar Straus Giroux
New York

For my parents, with love —A. A.

To Arne, for being the best piano teacher a child could wish for. Kind, inspiring, and always patient. —A. L.

To everyone who has heard of my famous younger brother, Wolfgang, but has never heard of me

—Nannerl Mozart

Papa always had a violin tucked under his chin. When his friends came to our home in Salzburg, they made music for the angels. I knew I had to make music, too.

“Please, Papa! Teach me to play the harpsichord.”

I climbed onto the wooden bench. Papa placed each of my fingers on a smooth ivory key. Using one finger at a time, I pressed down hard. Each key sang back to me in its own special voice.

I practiced for hours each day.

In no time, music poured out of me like water over the riverbanks in springtime. Confident. Wild. Carefree.

Wolfgang always wanted to do everything I did, so Papa taught him, too.

Within a few months, we were playing side by side, faster and faster, memorizing more and more difficult pieces.

By the time I was ten, Papa bragged that I was the best child musician in Europe.

He arranged for me to play in the concert halls of Munich, Linz, and Paris.

Wolfie came along to play the easier pieces.

At first, my hands shook. What if I made a mistake?

But each time we performed, applause filled the room.

By the time we reached Paris, my fears had disappeared.

We stopped in Vienna to perform for the Empress Maria Theresa.

Wolfie and I played blindfolded.

The audience begged for more. So much fuss over a silly trick that wasn't the least bit hard to do!

The empress was kinder than she looked. She sent us fancy clothes and filled Papa's pouch with gold coins.

Back in Salzburg, Papa gave us new pieces to play—more difficult and exciting than anything we had seen before.

I could hear the music before my fingers touched the keys. These notes needed me, and I needed them.

Together, we would bring their magic into the world.

Wolfie and I practiced all day.

Two bodies. Four hands. One perfect purpose.

Months later, we packed our valises again.

This time, we made a grand tour, playing in cities from Munich to London to Lyon.

During the long, bumpy carriage rides from town to town, Wolfie and I invented a magical kingdom. It had a secret language—and NO grown-ups.

I also did something else that was just a little bit naughty. When we were not practicing or performing, I wrote music.

At a concert in London, Wolfie played one of my sonatas. I curtsied shyly as the audience applauded. Wolfie beamed with pride.

But off to the side, Papa fumed. Girls were not allowed to compose. He ordered me never to write music again.

That night, I prayed for God to make me a boy.

Soon after we returned home, Papa planned our next tour.

But something was different. When I practiced, he didn't compliment the lift of my wrists or fuss over the crescendos in my sonatas.

"You and Mama will stay here. You are eighteen. Soon you will marry."

Marry? Music was my only love!

"Please, Papa! Let me come with you."

I played the most difficult pieces for him. Perfect! Every one!

Wolfie watched, helpless against Papa's power and fearful of his anger.

We both knew Papa's decision was final.

The day Papa and Wolfie set out for Italy, there was no music in my heart.

They were away for months or years at a time.

While they were gone, I wrote sonatas and concertos. I couldn't help it. The music in my head begged to be free.

Wolfie and I sent each other our compositions.

He said my work was brilliant. So was his.

Years later, Wolfie invited Papa and me to Munich to hear his new opera, *Idomeneo*.

But that was not the best part.

After Munich, we would perform together in Augsburg.

It had been years since Papa had allowed me to play in public.

Wolfie and I sat close, our arms weaving over and under each other in an elaborate dance across the keyboard.

My heart soared!

After the performance, Wolfie pulled me aside.

"Come with me to Vienna," he pleaded. "We could give concerts together again. Girls are writing music now. You could, too."

But it was not to be. A daughter could not disobey her father.

Once we returned home, Wolfie's letters came less frequently. Without word from my dear brother, it became harder for me to write music. My heart felt cold and empty.

Papa arranged for me to marry a man from St. Gilgen who had no love for music. Without music, my heart had no home.

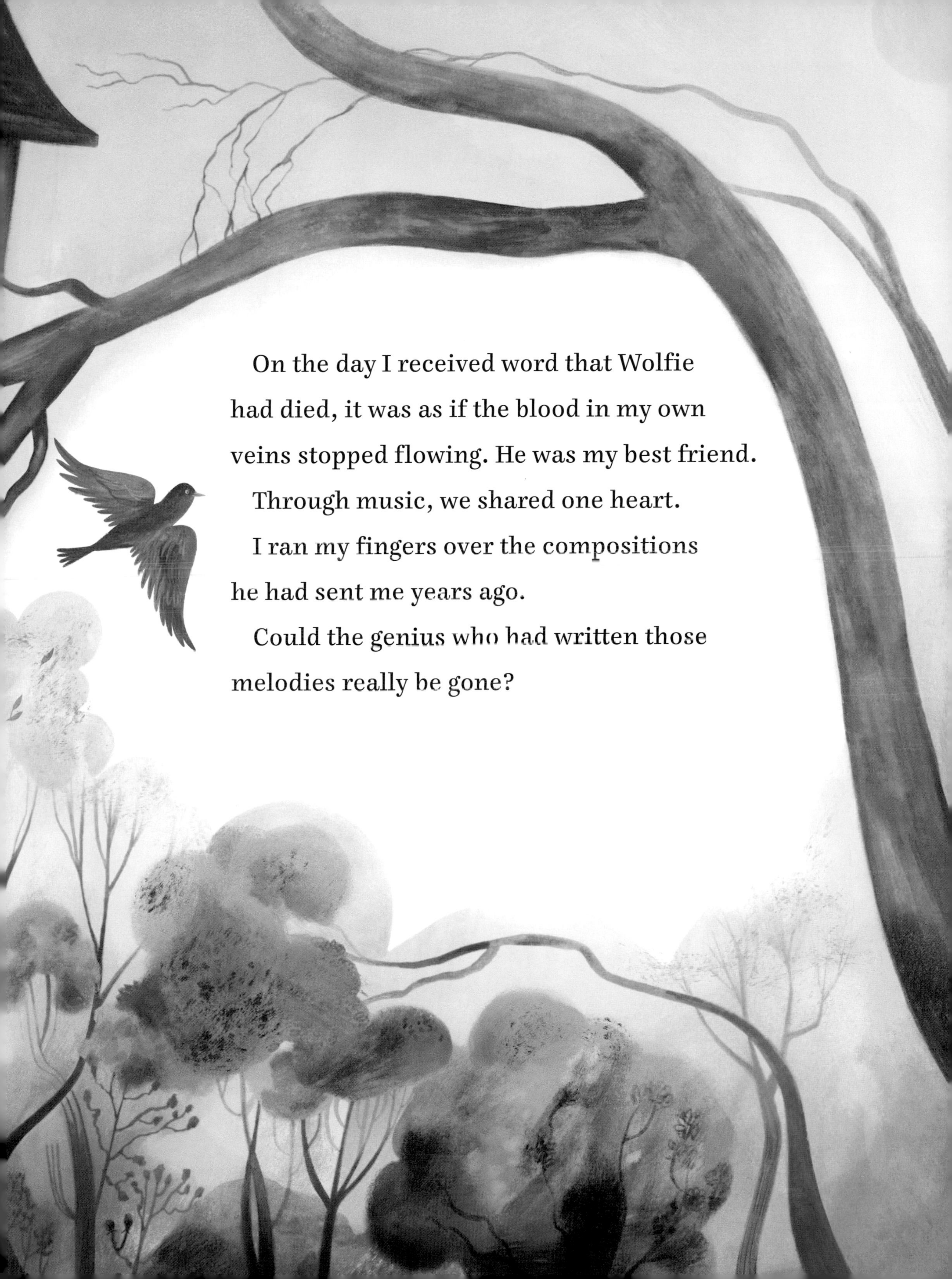

On the day I received word that Wolfie had died, it was as if the blood in my own veins stopped flowing. He was my best friend. Through music, we shared one heart.

I ran my fingers over the compositions he had sent me years ago.

Could the genius who had written those melodies really be gone?

I returned to Salzburg after my husband died.

It seemed ages since I had played the harpsichord.

But when I laid my fingers on the keys, music poured through my hands.

My heart had not forgotten its first true love.

I was, after all, a Mozart.

Fact or Fiction

I Am Mozart, Too is written in a style called "creative nonfiction." Creative nonfiction tells a story about events that really happened. Events that are true are called facts. But in this style of writing, it is understood that details may be added or changed to highlight important themes or ideas. These changes may be fiction, or not true to what really occurred.

Nannerl Mozart was a real person and a real musical genius. She really did travel and perform with her brother all across Europe. And she really was forced by her strict and domineering father to end her musical career when she was eighteen. These are facts.

Fiction means made-up. We don't know exactly how Nannerl or her family felt or what they thought or said. An author can only imagine these things based on what is known about the lives of the people in the story.

In *this* telling of Nannerl's story, some events have been exaggerated or changed to fit more easily into a picture book. For example, the Mozarts toured so many cities that some have been omitted here or not presented in order. Also, Nannerl and Wolfie probably never performed blindfolded, but they did show off their talent with similar stunts that would not have been as clear in the illustrations. Another example of a change is when Nannerl and Wolfie played together as adults. During this happy reunion, they played two separate keyboards. But in a book with pictures, the joy of playing together is conveyed more powerfully with the two of them sitting side by side.

We are not sure exactly which instrument Nannerl and Wolfie learned to play on, although it was most likely a harpsichord with either one or two keyboards. During their touring years, they played several different but similar instruments. The harpsichord, the clavichord, the pianoforte, and the piano were all common keyboard instruments of the time. It is often unknown which instrument they were playing at what time, and the book's illustrations do not distinguish between them.

After reading creative nonfiction, you may want to learn more about the subject of the story. You can learn more about Nannerl and her family in these and other books.

For the Love of Music: The Remarkable Story of Maria Anna Mozart by Elizabeth Rusch

Play, Mozart, Play! by Peter Sis

Who Was Wolfgang Amadeus Mozart? by Yona Zeldis McDonough

Why did Nannerl do everything her papa told her to?

Life for girls and women in eighteenth-century Europe was much different from today. Men, especially the father of the family, made all the important decisions. Girls and women were taught from an early age to be quiet and obedient. They depended on men to protect them and provide for them.

Nannerl was lucky to have had opportunities to travel and see the world when she was young. But when her papa pushed her aside to focus on Wolfie's career, there was little she could do. Perhaps some girls of the time would have disobeyed their fathers, but we have no evidence that Nannerl ever did.

Who was Wolfgang Mozart?

Like Nannerl, Wolfgang Mozart was a musical genius. His English nickname would probably have been Wolfie. He began writing music at age five and went on to write over 625 compositions, including many symphonies, concertos, operas, and other music still performed today. Because he was male, he was given opportunities to study, perform, and compose music throughout his life. Most people consider Wolfgang to be one of the greatest composers who ever lived.

Time Line

1751	Maria Anna Walburga Ignatia Mozart is born in Salzburg, Austria, on July 31. Her family calls her Nannerl.
1756	Nannerl's brother, Johannes Chrysostomus Wolfgangus Theophilus Mozart, is born on January 27. He is called Wolfgangerl and Woferl (Wolfie, in English).
1762	The Mozarts take their first performance tour.
1763	The Mozart family begins a three-and-a-half-year concert tour. Nannerl and Wolfgang become famous throughout Europe.
1769	Wolfgang and his father leave Nannerl and Mama home when they travel to Italy.
1777	Wolfgang and his mother leave Nannerl home when they tour Germany and France.
1778	Nannerl's mother, Maria Anna Pertl Mozart, dies in Paris.
1784	Nannerl marries at age thirty-three.
1787	Nannerl's father, Leopold Mozart, dies in Salzburg.
1791	Wolfgang dies on December 5 in Vienna. The cause of his death is still unclear.
1829	Nannerl dies in Salzburg on October 29. She was seventy-eight.

Glossary

composition—A written piece of music for voice, instrument(s), or both.

crescendo—A gradual increase in volume in a piece of music.

harpsichord—A keyboard musical instrument that produces sound by plucking metal strings when keys are pressed. It was popular from the 1500s through the mid-1700s.

opera—A story set to music, performed by costumed singers.

sonata—A composition that features one instrument, often accompanied by a piano.

Works Consulted

Books

Anderson, Emily, ed. *The Letters of Mozart and His Family*. Vol. 1. London: Macmillan, 1938.

Giordano, Luca Andrea. *Nannerl Mozart: The Destiny of the Forgotten Genius*. Rome: Aracn Editrice, 2011.

Glover, Jane. *Mozart's Women: His Family, His Friends, His Music*. New York: HarperCollins, 2005.

Sadie, Stanley. *Mozart: The Early Years, 1756–1781*. New York: Oxford University Press, 2006.

Siepmann, Jeremy. *Mozart: His Life & Music*. Naperville, IL: Sourcebooks, 2006.

Solomon, Maynard. *Mozart: A Life*. New York: HarperCollins, 1995.

Tapper, Thomas. *Mozart: The Story of a Little Boy and His Sister Who Gave Concerts*. Philadelphia: Theodore Presser, 1915.

Weeks, Marcus. *Mozart: The Boy Who Changed the World with His Music*. Washington, DC: National Geographic, 2007.

Online Sources

Medical Bag. "What Killed 'Em: Wolfgang Amadeus Mozart." September 12, 2012. www.medicalbag.com/what-killed-em/wolfgang-amadeus-mozart/article/486647/.

Milo, Sylvia. "The Lost Genius of Mozart's Sister." *Guardian*. September 8, 2015. www.theguardian.com/music/2015/sep/08/lost-genius-the-other-mozart-sister-nannerl.